Good Morning, God
Published by Apologia Press
a division of Apologia Educational Ministries, Inc.
1106 Meridian Plaza, Suite 220
Anderson, Indiana 46016
www.apologia.com

Manufactured in the USA
Printed by Moore Langen Printing
Terre Haute, Indiana
First Printing May 2010
ISBN: 978-1-935495-25-3

Illustrations: Alice Ratterree
Cover and book design: Alice Ratterree
www.aliceink.com

This book is dedicated to my seven incredible children:

Charles

Anderson

Savannah Anne

Molly

Elizabeth

Joseph

Benjamin

How to use this book

This book is designed for children age one to eight years old. Ideally, this book will help your child fall in love with our heavenly Father by thinking about Him from sunrise to sunset. The hope is that this book will introduce children to the simple and wonderful ways we can worship God daily and inspire them to enjoy the Lord with their entire being all through the day. The prayers for each day are meant to encourage your child to consider his or her relationship with Jesus and respond with childlike faith.

There are several ways this book can be used as a discipleship tool to accomplish these goals. The most basic is to simply read the book as a story. At the end of the book are suggested questions you can ask and activities that you can do with your children. The questions and activities are organized by the theme of each day in the book. The purpose of each question and activity is to help your child relate his or her own life with the thoughts, actions, and prayers of the main character in the story. You don't have to ask all the questions or do all the activities in any one sitting. You can choose to concentrate on a few of the items listed for a given day.

If you really get into it, you can choose to read the book at least once every day from Sunday to the following Sunday. On the first Sunday, you can read the scriptures listed, then have a discussion with your child using the questions for that day. On Monday, you can read the book again and ask the questions, read the scripture, and do some or all of the activities for Monday. You can continue this plan for Tuesday, Wednesday, Thursday, Friday, Saturday, and the following Sunday. On the second Sunday, you can ask the suggested questions and do the recommended activities listed on the last page of Sunday Questions and Activities. Following this plan would result in reading the book eight straight days and would basically make the book a mini-curriculum and a literal application of Deuteronomy 6:6-7, where parents are told to impress these commands on their children's hearts and talk about them when you sit at home, when you walk along the road, when you lie down, and when you get up.

Now sit back, relax, and enjoy the time reading to your little ones. And may God bless you and your children for a thousand generations or until Jesus returns.

These commands
that I give you today
are to be upon your hearts.

Impress them on your children.
Talk about them
when you sit at home
and when you walk along the road,
when you lie down
and when you get up.

DEUTERONOMY 6:6-7

Good morning, God. Today is *Sunday*. I wake up with lots of energy.
I worship God with my family and with all of my *being*.

Mom and Dad teach me when I'm sitting, when I'm standing, and especially when I'm at *church*.

On the porch, I think about *heaven*.

At bedtime, I pray to God. I say, "Jesus, I hope you come back soon.
I want to live with you forever. In Jesus' name. Amen."

Good night, Sunday. Good night, God.

Good morning, God. Today is *Monday*. I wake up with lots of energy.
I worship God with my family and with all of my *heart*.

Mom and Dad teach me when I'm sitting, when I'm standing,
and especially when I'm *running*.

In the school room,
I color a *picture*.

At bedtime, I pray to God. I say, "Thank you, God, for Mom, Dad, and my brothers and sisters. In Jesus' name. Amen."

Good night, Monday. Good night, God.

Good morning, God. Today is *Tuesday*. I wake up with lots of energy.
I worship God with my family and with all of my *mind*.

Mom and Dad teach me when I'm sitting, when I'm standing, and especially when I'm *jumping*.

In the kitchen, I make a *sandwich*.

At bedtime, I pray to God. I say, "Thank you, God, for making me alive and loving me. In Jesus' name. Amen."

Good night, Tuesday.
Good night, God.

Good morning, God. Today is *Wednesday*. I wake up with lots of energy.
I worship God with my family and with all of my *body*.

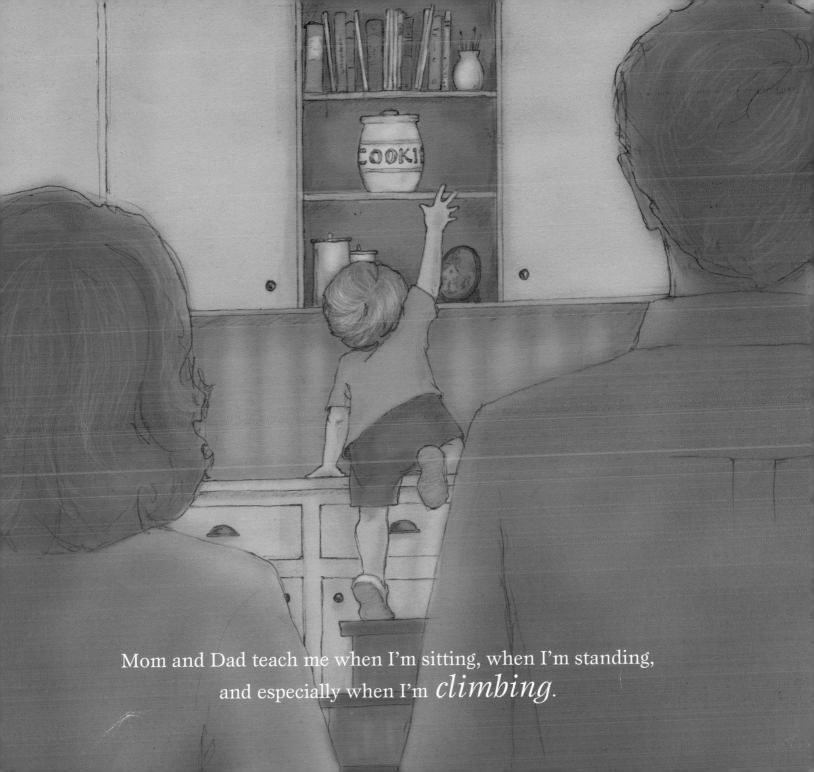

Mom and Dad teach me when I'm sitting, when I'm standing,
and especially when I'm *climbing*.

In the family room, I read a *book*.

At bedtime, I pray to God.

I say, "Heavenly Father, forgive me of my sins.

In Jesus' name. Amen."

Good night, Wednesday.

Good night, God.

Good morning, God. Today is *Thursday*.
I wake up with lots of energy. I worship God
with my family and with all of my *soul*.

Mom and Dad teach me when I'm sitting, when I'm standing, and especially when I'm *walking*.

In the toy room, I play with my *brother and sister*.

At bedtime, I pray to
God. I say, "Thank
you, God, for sending
Jesus to earth to die on
the cross and save me.
In Jesus' name. Amen."

Good night, Thursday.
Good night, God.

Good morning, God. Today is *Friday*. I wake up with lots of energy.
I worship God with my family and with all of my *thoughts*.

Mom and Dad teach me when I'm sitting, when I'm standing, and especially when I'm *listening*.

In the back yard, I climb a *tree*.

At bedtime, I pray to God.
I say, "Thank you, God, that
Jesus loves me so much.
In Jesus' name. Amen."

Good night, Friday.
Good night, God.

Good morning, God. Today is *Saturday*. I wake up with lots of energy.
I worship God with my family and with all of my *strength*.

Mom and Dad teach me when I'm sitting, when I'm standing, and especially when I'm *quiet*.

In the driveway, I ride my *bike*.

At bedtime, I pray to God. I say, "Thank you, God, that Jesus rose from the dead and went back to heaven. In Jesus' name. Amen."

Good night, Saturday.
Good night, God.

Good morning, God. Today is *Sunday*. I wake up with lots of energy.
I worship God with my family and with all of my *being*.

Mom and Dad teach me when I'm sitting, when I'm standing, and especially when I'm at *church*.

On the porch, I think about *heaven*.

At bedtime, I pray to
God. I say, "Jesus, I
hope you come back
soon. I want to live
with you forever.
In Jesus' name.
Amen."

Good night, Sunday.
Good night, God.

What are some of the ways you can worship God?

What is the church?

Read Revelation 21:1-7.

Imagine how things will be "new" in heaven.

Whom do you look forward to seeing again in heaven?

What do you want to know about heaven?

Read 1 Thessalonians 4:13-18.

What do you think it will be like to meet the Lord in the air?

Draw a picture of a heart.

Read Matthew 6:19-21.

What is something you treasure?

How can you love God with all your heart?

What is your favorite thing to do in school?

Draw a picture of your dad, mom, brothers, and sisters.

Why are you thankful for your family?

How can you be a good brother or sister?

How can you love God with all of your mind?

What does a brain do?

Name some animals God created that jump.

Can you jump like them?

What kind of sandwich do you like to eat?
Can you make it by yourself?

What does it mean to be alive?

Read John 3:16.

Give some examples of how God loves you.

Draw a human body and label the parts (for example, head, hands, legs, and eyes).

Take a picture of yourself and print it out.

Read 1 Corinthians 6:19-20.

How can you take care of your body?

What are some things you like to climb?

What are your favorite books to read?

What is sin? Have you ever sinned?

How can your sins be forgiven?

What is a soul?

How can you love God with all your soul?

Take a walk and look at all the wonderful things God created.

Talk about what you would probably see on a walk in the mountains compared to a walk on the beach.

Read Philippians 2:5-11.

Why did Jesus have to die to save you?

What are some games you like to play?

Have a family night and play a game together.

What do you like to think about?

Read Philippians 4:8.

What is an example of a noble thought, a praiseworthy thought, or a pure thought?

Draw a picture of an ear.

Why did God give you ears?

Do you prefer to listen to songs or stories?

What are some things you shouldn't listen to?

What are some ways Jesus loves you?

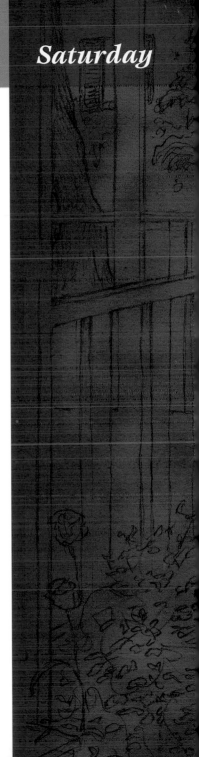

What does it mean to love God with all your strength?

Who were some strong men mentioned in the Bible?

Read Psalm 23 and 46:10.

How can being quiet help you know, love, and worship God?

Where are some places that you need to be quiet?

Go on a bike ride.

Read Acts 1:9-11.

Draw a picture of Jesus ascending into heaven.

What does it mean to be a human being?

What does it mean to be made in God's image?

Read Psalm 139.

How are you fearfully and wonderfully made?

Look at pictures of when you were a baby.

Read John 14:1-6.

Draw a picture of the place you think Jesus is preparing for you.

What does forever mean?